Claude Monet (1840–1926)
The Japanese Footbridge, 1899
Oil on canvas, 81.3 x 101.6 cm
National Gallery of Art, Washington
Gift of Victoria Nebeker Coberly, in memory of her son
John W. Mudd, and Walter H. and Leonore Annenberg 1992.9.1
© Board of Trustees, National Gallery of Art, Washington

GALISON
NEW YORK
WWW.GALISON.COM

Edgar Degas (1834–1917)
Four Dancers, c. 1899
Oil on canvas, 151.1 x 180.2 cm
National Gallery of Art, Washington
Chester Dale Collection 1963.10.122
© Board of Trustees, National Gallery of Art, Washington

GALISON
NEW YORK
WWW.GALISON.COM

Vincent van Gogh (1853–1890)
Roses, 1890
Oil on canvas, 71 x 90 cm
National Gallery of Art, Washington
Gift of Pamela Harriman in memory of W. Averell Harriman 1991.67.1
© Board of Trustees, National Gallery of Art, Washington

NATIONAL GALLERY OF ART, WASHINGTON

GALISON
NEW YORK
WWW.GALISON.COM

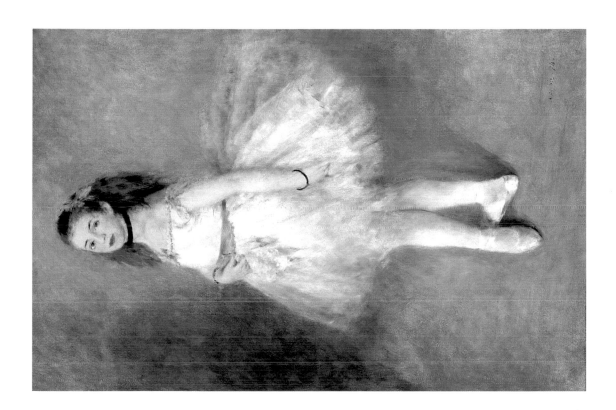

Auguste Renoir (1841–1919)
The Dancer, 1874
Oil on canvas, 142.5 x 94.5 cm
National Gallery of Art, Washington
Widener Collection 1942.9.72
© Board of Trustees, National Gallery of Art, Washington

GALISON
NEW YORK
WWW.GALISON.COM

Leonardo da Vinci (1452–1519)
Ginevra de' Benci (obverse), c. 1474
Oil on panel, 38.1 x 37 cm
National Gallery of Art, Washington
Ailsa Mellon Bruce Fund 1967.6.1.a
© Board of Trustees, National Gallery of Art, Washington

Childe Hassam (1859–1935)
Poppies, Isles of Shoals, 1891
Oil on canvas, 50.2 x 61 cm
National Gallery of Art, Washington
Gift (Partial and Promised) of Margaret and Raymond Horowitz 1997.135.1
© Board of Trustees, National Gallery of Art, Washington

NATIONAL GALLERY OF ART, WASHINGTON

GALISON
NEW YORK
WWW.GALISON.COM

Mary Cassatt (1844–1926)
Children Playing on the Beach, 1884
Oil on canvas, 97.4 x 74.2 cm
National Gallery of Art, Washington
Ailsa Mellon Bruce Collection 1970.17.19
© Board of Trustees, National Gallery of Art, Washington

GALISON
NEW YORK
WWW.GALISON.COM

Jan Davidsz. de Heem (1606–1683/1684)
Vase of Flowers, c. 1660
Oil on canvas, 69.6 x 56.5 cm
National Gallery of Art, Washington
Andrew W. Mellon Fund 1961.6.1
© Board of Trustees, National Gallery of Art, Washington

NATIONAL GALLERY OF ART, WASHINGTON

Claude Monet (1840–1926)
Woman with a Parasol—Madame Monet and Her Son, 1875
Oil on canvas, 100 x 81 cm
National Gallery of Art, Washington
Collection of Mr. and Mrs. Paul Mellon 1983.1.29
© Board of Trustees, National Gallery of Art, Washington

GALISON
NEW YORK
WWW.GALISON.COM

James McNeill Whistler (1834–1903)
Symphony in White, No. 1: The White Girl, 1862
Oil on canvas, 213 x 107.9 cm
National Gallery of Art, Washington
Harris Whittemore Collection 1943.6.2
© Board of Trustees, National Gallery of Art, Washington

NATIONAL GALLERY OF ART, WASHINGTON

GALISON
NEW YORK
WWW.GALISON.COM

Edouard Manet (1832–1883)
Flowers in a Crystal Vase, c. 1882
Oil on canvas, 32.6 x 24.3 cm
National Gallery of Art, Washington
Ailsa Mellon Bruce Collection 1970.17.37
© Board of Trustees, National Gallery of Art, Washington

NATIONAL GALLERY OF ART, WASHINGTON

Henri de Toulouse-Lautrec (1864–1901)
Jane Avril, 1899
5-color lithograph (poster)
National Gallery of Art, Washington
Rosenwald Collection 1953.6.137
© Board of Trustees, National Gallery of Art, Washington

GALISON
NEW YORK
WWW.GALISON.COM

Johannes Vermeer (1632–1675)
Girl with the Red Hat, c. 1665/1666
Oil on panel, 22.8 x 18 cm
National Gallery of Art, Washington
Andrew W. Mellon Collection 1937.1.53
© Board of Trustees, National Gallery of Art, Washington

GALISON
NEW YORK
WWW.GALISON.COM

Martin Johnson Heade (1819–1904)
Giant Magnolias on a Blue Velvet Cloth, c. 1890
Oil on canvas, 38.4 x 61.5 cm
National Gallery of Art, Washington
Gift of The Circle of the National Gallery of Art
in Commemoration of its 10th Anniversary 1996.14.1
© Board of Trustees, National Gallery of Art, Washington

NATIONAL GALLERY OF ART, WASHINGTON

Raphael (1483–1520)
The Small Cowper Madonna, c. 1505
Oil on panel, 59.5 x 44 cm
National Gallery of Art, Washington
Widener Collection 1942.9.57
© Board of Trustees, National Gallery of Art, Washington

GALISON
NEW YORK
WWW.GALISON.COM

Auguste Renoir (1841–1919)
A Girl with a Watering Can, 1876
Oil on canvas, 100.3 x 73.2 cm
National Gallery of Art, Washington
Chester Dale Collection 1963.10.206
© Board of Trustees, National Gallery of Art, Washington

GALISON
NEW YORK
WWW.GALISON.COM

Paul Cézanne (1839–1906)
Houses in Provence, c. 1880
Oil on canvas, 65 x 81.3 cm
National Gallery of Art, Washington
Collection of Mr. and Mrs. Paul Mellon 1973.68.1
© Board of Trustees, National Gallery of Art, Washington

GALISON
NEW YORK
WWW.GALISON.COM

William Michael Harnett (1848–1892)
The Old Violin, 1886
Oil on canvas, 96.5 x 60 cm
National Gallery of Art, Washington
Gift of Mr. and Mrs. Richard Mellon Scaife in honor of Paul Mellon 1993.15.1
© Board of Trustees, National Gallery of Art, Washington

GALISON
NEW YORK
WWW.GALISON.COM

Jean Siméon Chardin (1699–1779)
Soap Bubbles, probably 1733/1734
Oil on canvas, 93 x 74.6 cm
National Gallery of Art, Washington
Gift of Mrs. John W. Simpson 1942.5.1
© Board of Trustees, National Gallery of Art, Washington

NATIONAL GALLERY OF ART, WASHINGTON

Vincent van Gogh (1853–1890)
Farmhouse in Provence, 1888
Oil on canvas, 46.1 x 60.9 cm
National Gallery of Art, Washington
Ailsa Mellon Bruce Collection 1970.17.34
© Board of Trustees, National Gallery of Art, Washington

NATIONAL GALLERY OF ART, WASHINGTON

Winslow Homer (1836–1910)
Salt Kettle, *Bermuda*, 1899
Watercolor over graphite, 35.5 x 53.3 cm
National Gallery of Art, Washington
Gift of Ruth K. Henschel in memory of her husband,
Charles R. Henschel 1975.92.15
© Board of Trustees, National Gallery of Art, Washington

GALISON
NEW YORK
WWW.GALISON.COM

Jean-Honoré Fragonard (1732–1806)
A Young Girl Reading, c. 1776
Oil on canvas, 81.1 x 64.8 cm
National Gallery of Art, Washington
Gift of Mrs. Mellon Bruce in memory of her father, Andrew W. Mellon 1961.16.1
© Board of Trustees, National Gallery of Art, Washington

NATIONAL GALLERY OF ART, WASHINGTON

GALISON
NEW YORK
WWW.GALISON.COM

Georges Seurat (1859–1891)
The Lighthouse at Honfleur, 1886
Oil on canvas, 66.7 x 81.9 cm
National Gallery of Art, Washington
Collection of Mr. and Mrs. Paul Mellon 1983.1.33
© Board of Trustees, National Gallery of Art, Washington

NATIONAL GALLERY OF ART, WASHINGTON

GALISON
NEW YORK
WWW.GALISON.COM

George Romney (1734–1802)
Miss Juliana Willoughby, 1781–1783
Oil on canvas, 92.1 x 71.5 cm
National Gallery of Art, Washington
Andrew W. Mellon Collection 1937.1.104
© Board of Trustees, National Gallery of Art, Washington

John Constable (1776–1837)
Wivenhoe Park, Essex, 1816
Oil on canvas, 56.1 x 101.2 cm
National Gallery of Art, Washington
Widener Collection 1942.9.10
© Board of Trustees, National Gallery of Art, Washington

NATIONAL GALLERY OF ART, WASHINGTON

GALISON
NEW YORK
WWW.GALISON.COM

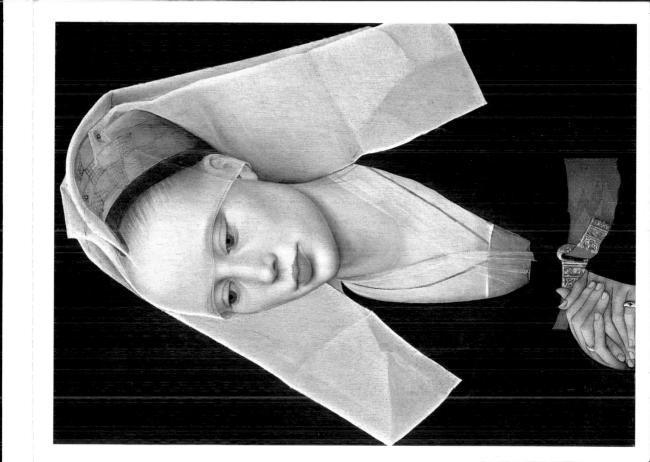

Rogier van der Weyden (1399/1400–1464)
Portrait of a Lady, c. 1460
Oil on panel, 34 x 25.5 cm
National Gallery of Art, Washington
Andrew W. Mellon Collection 1937.1.44
© Board of Trustees, National Gallery of Art, Washington

NATIONAL GALLERY OF ART, WASHINGTON

GALISON
NEW YORK
WWW.GALISON.COM

Masolino da Panicale (1383–probably 1440/1447)
The Annunciation, probably 1425/1430
Tempera (and possibly oil glazes) on panel, 148.8 x 151.1 cm
National Gallery of Art, Washington
Andrew W. Mellon Collection 1937.1.16
© Board of Trustees, National Gallery of Art, Washington

NATIONAL GALLERY OF ART, WASHINGTON

GALISON
NEW YORK
WWW.GALISON.COM

Jan Brueghel the Elder (1568–1625)
River Landscape, 1607
Oil on copper, 20.7 x 32.1 cm
National Gallery of Art, Washington
Patrons' Permanent Fund and Nell and Robert Weidenhammer Fund 2000.4.1
© Board of Trustees, National Gallery of Art, Washington

NATIONAL GALLERY OF ART, WASHINGTON

GALISON
NEW YORK
WWW.GALISON.COM